EVERYTHING SPORTS

# EVERYTHING FOOTBALL

SYDNEY NEWTON

A Crabtree Canopy Book

Crabtree Publishing
crabtreebooks.com

EVERYTHING SPORTS

**Author**
Sydney Newton

**Contributors**
Jennifer Rivkin
Rachel Stuckey
Jaime Winters

**Editors**
Sissy McGonagal
Crystal Sikkens

**Proofreader**
Kathy Middleton

**Design**
Margaret Salter

**Production manager**
Candice Campbell

**Images**
Newscom: p. 19 (top right)
Wikimedia Commons: p. 5 (top), 6 (inset), 7, 8 (all), 9 (bottom), 11 (all), 12 (all), 13 (top right), 16, 17 (middle), 19 (all), 20 (bottom left and bottom right), 21 (middle right, bottom), 22 (all), 23 (top, middle left, bottom), 24, 25 (all), 27 (bottom), 28 (top and bottom inset), 29, 31 (top inset), 34 (inset), 37 (all), 38, 39 (top and bottom), 40 (all), 41 (top and middle), 42, 43 (main), 45 (right), 47 (top right main), 49, 50 (top), 51 (all), 52, 53 (top right), 54 (right), 55 (top and bottom), 57 (left), 58 (left), 59 (bottom right), 60 (left), 61 (bottom right)
Shutterstock: p. 46 (top) MPH Photos; 4 (bottom), 14 (bottom), 30 (bottom), Joseph Sohm; 32 (bottom) Jai Agnish; 26 (left), 46 (top right) Jeff Bukowski; 44 (top left) meunierd; 18 (bottom) Debby Wong; 48 (main left) Sterling Munksgard; 36 (right) Gavin Napier; 20 (middle left) Jamie Lamor Thompson; 59 (top) Grindstone Media Group; 35 (top) Brian Friedman; 41 (bottom) Mauricio Fernandes; 35 (bottom) lev radin; 34 (background) Marcus E Jones; 61 (top left) Debby Wong; 31 (bottom) WoodysPhotos; 17 (top right) Ringo Chiu; 20 (top right) Ringo Chiu; 17 (bottom) Gregory Reed; 33 (middle left) kovop; title page Ringo Chiu; front cover Steve Jacobson
All other images: Shutterstock.com

## Crabtree Publishing

crabtreebooks.com 800-387-7650

In Canada: We acknowledge the financial support of the Government of Canada through the Canada Book Fund for our publishing activities.

Hardcover 978-1-0398-8055-9
Ebook (pdf) 978-1-0398-8175-4
Epub 978-1-0398-8295-9

**Published in Canada**
**Crabtree Publishing**
616 Welland Avenue
St. Catharines, Ontario
L2M 5V6

**Published in the United States**
**Crabtree Publishing**
347 Fifth Avenue
Suite 1402-145
New York, NY 10016

**Library and Archives Canada Cataloguing in Publication**
Available at the Library and Archives Canada

**Library of Congress Cataloging-in-Publication Data**
Available at the Library of Congress

Printed in the U.S.A./CP072026

# CONTENTS

INTRODUCTION

# FOOTBALL AROUND THE WORLD

Football is the most popular sport in the United States. It is played at multiple levels and adored by fans. Professionally, the National Football League (NFL) is the premier North American league. Others include the Canadian Football League (CFL), as well as non-professional college football leagues.

**FAST FACT**

**Over 18 million viewers tune into the 272 NFL games broadcasted on TV during regular season play.**

## North American Ball

The International Federation of American Football (IFAF) governs national football associations in over 70 different countries. Many countries, such as Germany and Australia, have national teams and compete in international championships. There are also some professional leagues in Europe and other regions.

*In flag football, players cannot be **tackled**. Opponents must instead remove a flag or belt attached to a player.*

## Geared Up

Football is a contact sport and is usually played wearing padding and helmets. Another version of the game is called flag football. The only equipment needed is a belt with two flags attached. Opposing players end the play by grabbing or tearing off an opponent's flag. Flag football is usually a recreational sport that people of all **genders** play. The International Women's Flag Football Association hosts tournaments around the world.

## Footie and Football

Around the world, the name football causes some confusion. Outside of North America, football, or "footie" refers to the game of soccer. North American football is called American or gridiron football. The name gridiron came from the appearance of the original football fields, which had lines that ran the length and width of the field. The field looks like a kind of grill used for cooking called a gridiron.

CHAPTER 1

# THE BIRTH OF FOOTBALL

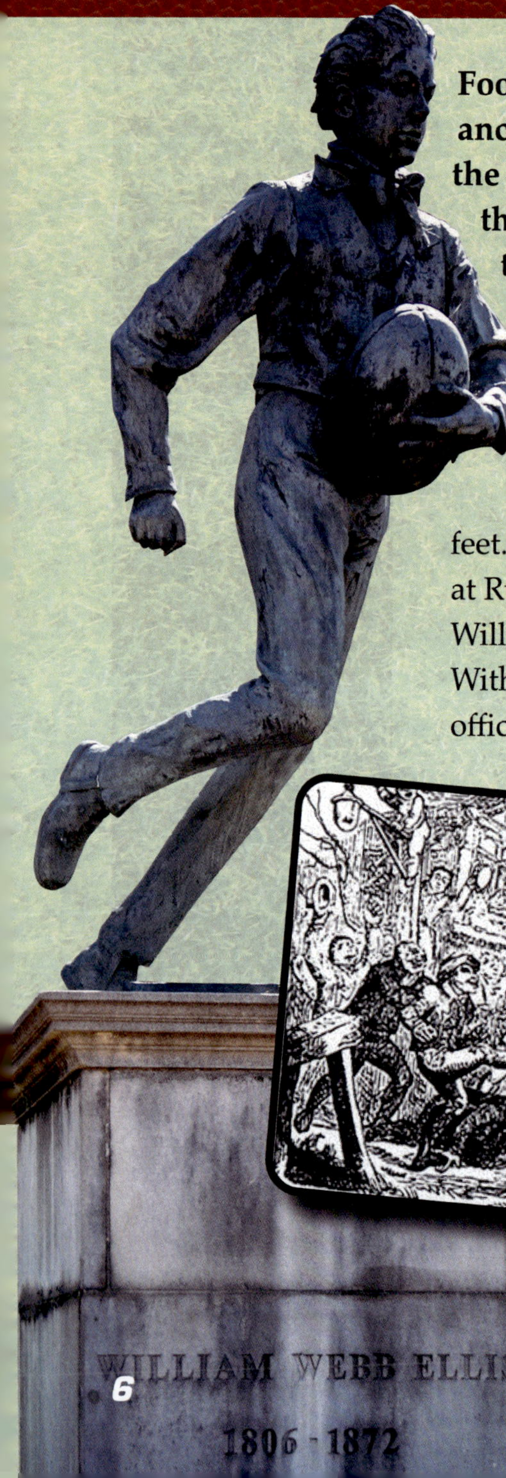


Football-type games go back at least as far as ancient Greece and Rome. These games are the ancestors of soccer and rugby, which led to the birth of football. Historians believe that the games spread with the Roman empire, especially in Britain.

## The Rugby School

By the 1600s, a soccer-like game had developed. Players could only touch the ball with their feet. The big change that led to football came in 1823, at Rugby School in England, when a player named William Webb Ellis grabbed the ball and ran with it. Within a few years, running with the ball became an official part of rugby.

### FAST FACT

**About 1,000 years ago, British boys were playing a tackling game using an inflated cow bladder as a ball. These games were so rough that players could be seriously injured or even killed.**

## Game Changer

Walter Chauncey Camp was an American football player and coach who became known as the "father of football." Active from the 1870s through the early 1920s, Camp made significant changes to the rules of soccer and rugby helping to create modern American football. Camp invented the **line of scrimmage**, where teams would begin each new play after the previous one had ended. He is also credited with lowering the number of players from 25 to 11 per team, the **system of downs** that each play takes place in, and the **snap-back** that starts each new play. He even set up a new scoring system and created the offensive backfield, which consists of a quarterback, two halfbacks, and a fullback.

*Walter Camp studied medicine and worked in the watchmaking business, but his passion was football. He played, coached, and wrote many of the rules. Camp was inducted into the College Hall of Fame as a coach.*

## Safety? Not So Much

By the late 1800s, Camp's new rules for football had caused the game's popularity to skyrocket. So did injuries. Originally, football was played without any safety equipment at all. In an Army-Navy game in 1893, the U.S. Naval Academy team football star, Joseph Reeves, wore one of the first padded caps.

In 1896, player George Barclay came up with a design that included straps that allowed the helmet to close tightly around his head and protect his ears. Leather helmets ruled the game until helmets made of plastic appeared in the mid 1940s. These eventually became standard equipment.

*Leather football helmets had little padding and absorbed heat, making them hot and uncomfortable to wear.*

*The first recorded game of North American football took place on November 6, 1869. The contest was between two universities: Rutgers and Princeton. Rutgers beat Princeton 6 to 4.*

## Famous Plays

Before the **forward pass** was brought to the game, **mass-momentum** plays were often used to move the ball forward. The most famous of these plays was called the flying wedge. The offensive team would form into a V-formation and charge the defense. They used their momentum, and other brutal means, to plow through or over the defensive line. The flying wedge was originally a military strategy to move men forward in battle. On the football field it was eventually banned because of deaths and injuries.

*Today, helmets are expertly engineered, providing much more safety and comfort. Some even incorporate technology like radio receivers, enabling players to hear calls and plays.*

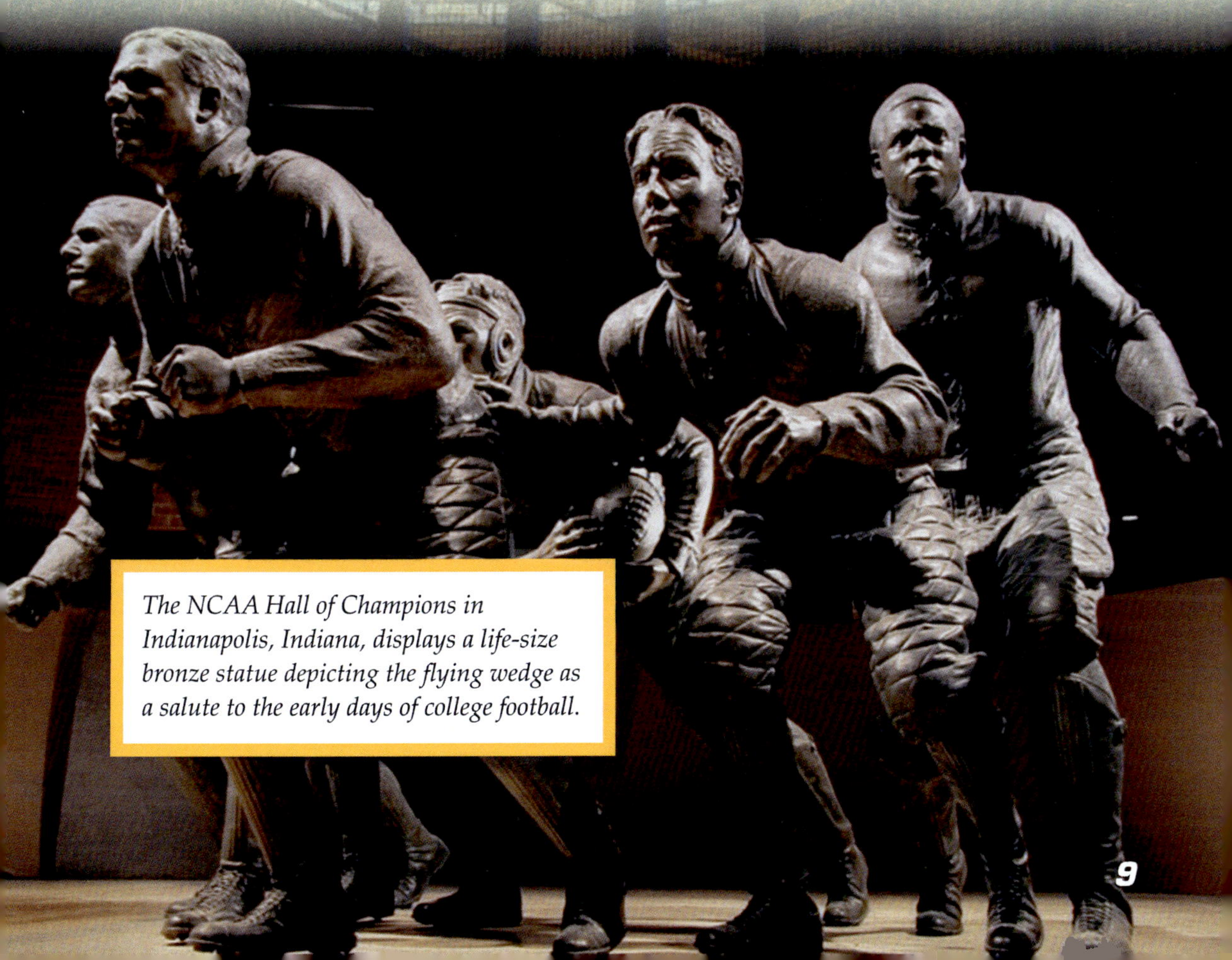

*The NCAA Hall of Champions in Indianapolis, Indiana, displays a life-size bronze statue depicting the flying wedge as a salute to the early days of college football.*

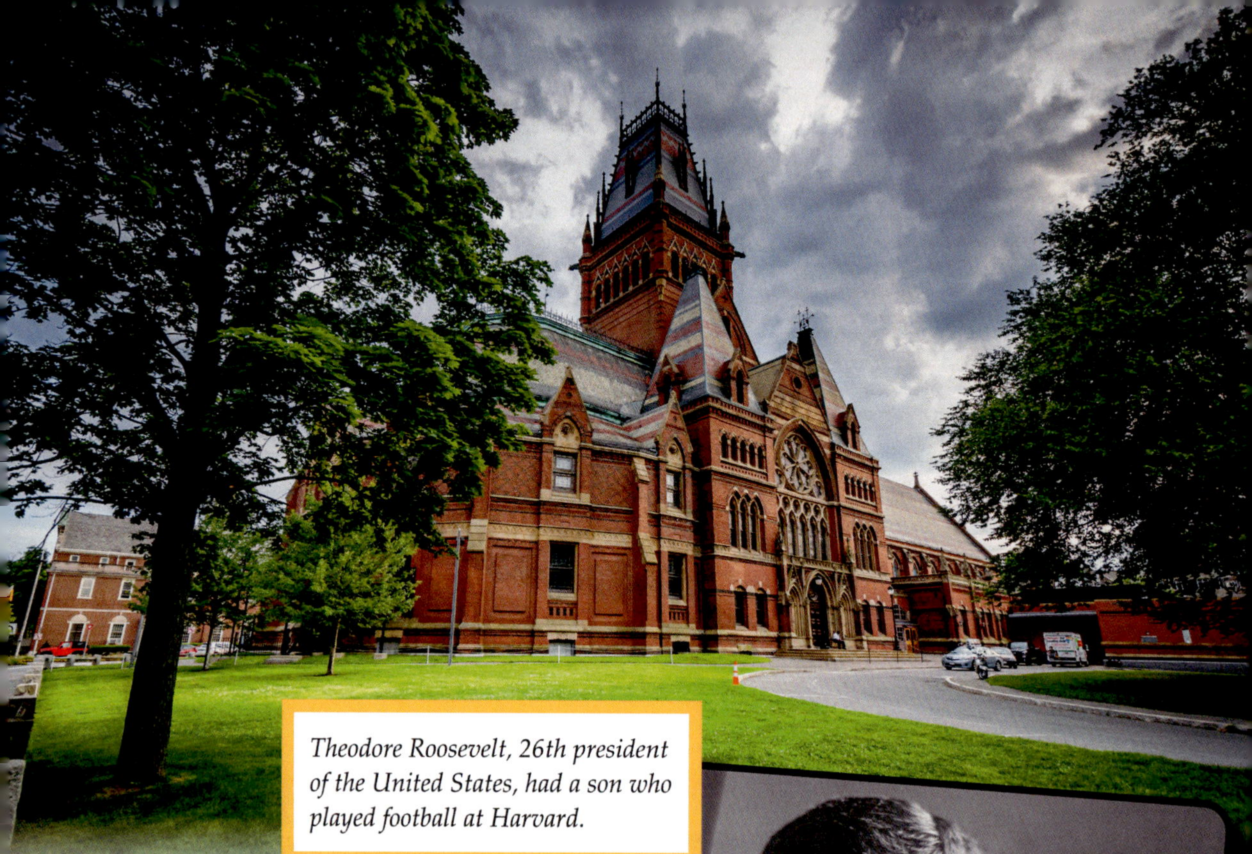

*Theodore Roosevelt, 26th president of the United States, had a son who played football at Harvard.*

## Rule Changes

In 1905, 18 players were killed and 149 serious injuries took place in games played nationwide. That same year, U.S. President Theodore "Teddy" Roosevelt arranged a meeting of officials from Harvard, Yale, and Princeton. President Roosevelt began his safety campaign with these schools because they were the top football schools at the time.

## Change or Be Banned

Unfortunately, Roosevelt's meeting did not lead to much change. This lack of action led Henry MacCracken, head of New York University, to organize a meeting of 13 schools. Amid cries from various groups to ban football outright, this meeting led to a decision to attempt to reform the sport to make it safer. Afterward, invitations to all football-playing institutions were sent out. On December 28, 1905, 62 schools came together to create a committee to standardize safer rules for the sport. The committee officially established itself as the Intercollegiate Athletic Association of the United States (IAAUS) on March 31, 1906.

Henry MacCracken

### Contact Rules

Since protective equipment was still new, the only way to make the game safer was to minimize the number of collisions. Rules were introduced that limited contact. The most important was the creation of the forward pass. **Roughing the passer** was brought into the rulebook in 1914 as the sport's popularity continued to grow.

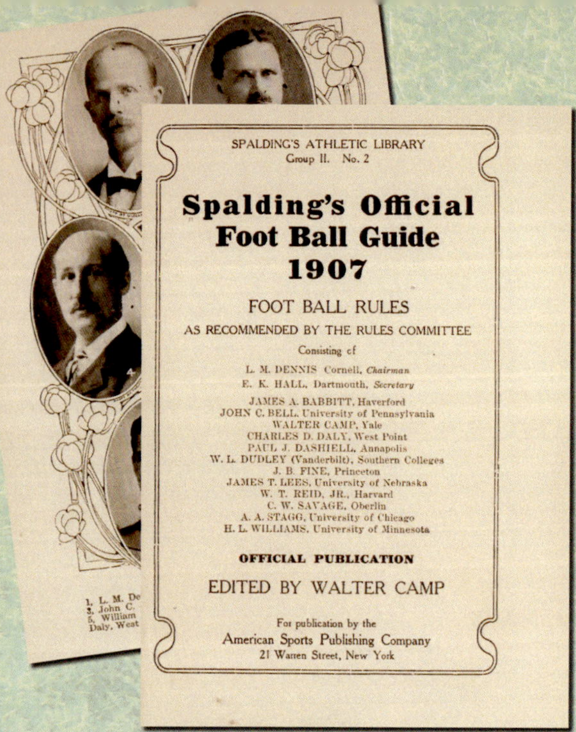

SPALDING'S ATHLETIC LIBRARY
Group II. No. 2

**Spalding's Official Foot Ball Guide 1907**

FOOT BALL RULES

AS RECOMMENDED BY THE RULES COMMITTEE

Consisting of

L. M. DENNIS, Cornell, *Chairman*
E. K. HALL, Dartmouth, *Secretary*
JAMES A. BABBITT, Haverford
JOHN C. BELL, University of Pennsylvania
WALTER CAMP, Yale
CHARLES D. DALY, West Point
PAUL J. DASHIELL, Annapolis
W. L. DUDLEY (Vanderbilt), Southern Colleges
J. B. FINE, Princeton
JAMES T. LEES, University of Nebraska
W. T. REID, JR., Harvard
C. W. SAVAGE, Oberlin
A. A. STAGG, University of Chicago
H. L. WILLIAMS, University of Minnesota

**OFFICIAL PUBLICATION**

EDITED BY WALTER CAMP

For publication by the
American Sports Publishing Company
21 Warren Street, New York

## Game Guide

In 1907, one of the first jobs of the new athletic association was to put together a football guide. The most significant rule change was the legalization of the forward pass. This made football the game we recognize today. Other changes included shortening the length of games, and allowing teams to gain 10 yards instead of five for a **first down**.

*The first footballs were round, much like soccer balls. They grew more oval in shape after the forward pass was added to the game in 1906.*

## Game Tested

Although a few teams had experimented with it previously, the first legal forward pass happened on September 5, 1906, during a game between St. Louis University and Carroll College. St. Louis quarterback Bradbury Robinson had tried it once unsuccessfully, but on his second attempt, the ball was caught by his teammate Jack Schneider. Eddie Cochems, the St. Louis coach, loved it so much that he is often called the "father of the forward pass."

*Robinson threw a 20-yard touchdown pass to his teammate Schneider, helping to secure their win over Carroll College 22-0. This first forward pass stunned both players and fans.*

CHAPTER 2

# COLLEGE BALL GLORY

**As the rules became more definite and the game became safer, college football's popularity soared across the country. The number of teams grew quickly, forming Conferences and staging season ending events called bowl games.**

## *The Big Ten*

The Big Ten Conference is the oldest college football division. It was formed in 1896 and includes teams from the Midwest and Mid-Atlantic. At first, it was made up of 10 major research universities, but later grew to 18. Historic **rivalries** between teams are an important part of the Big Ten's game scheduling.

### FAST FACT

**Many bowl games start with a parade. The floats in the Tournament of Roses Parade are famous for using more than 18 million fresh flowers!**

*The Rose Bowl is usually played on New Year's Day. Held in Passadena, CA, it is the highest-attended college playoff game.*

## The NCAA

Today, there are over 70 college football conferences. The National Collegiate Athletic Association (NCAA) is an organization that governs college athletics in the U.S. It groups teams into divisions based on size, budget, number of athletic scholarships, and level of training facilities available. There are groups within the divisions to make sure teams with the same level of talent play each other. The Division I Football Bowl Subdivision (FBS) is the highest level of college football. It includes the best-of-the-best college teams and has the most **scholarships** to offer players.

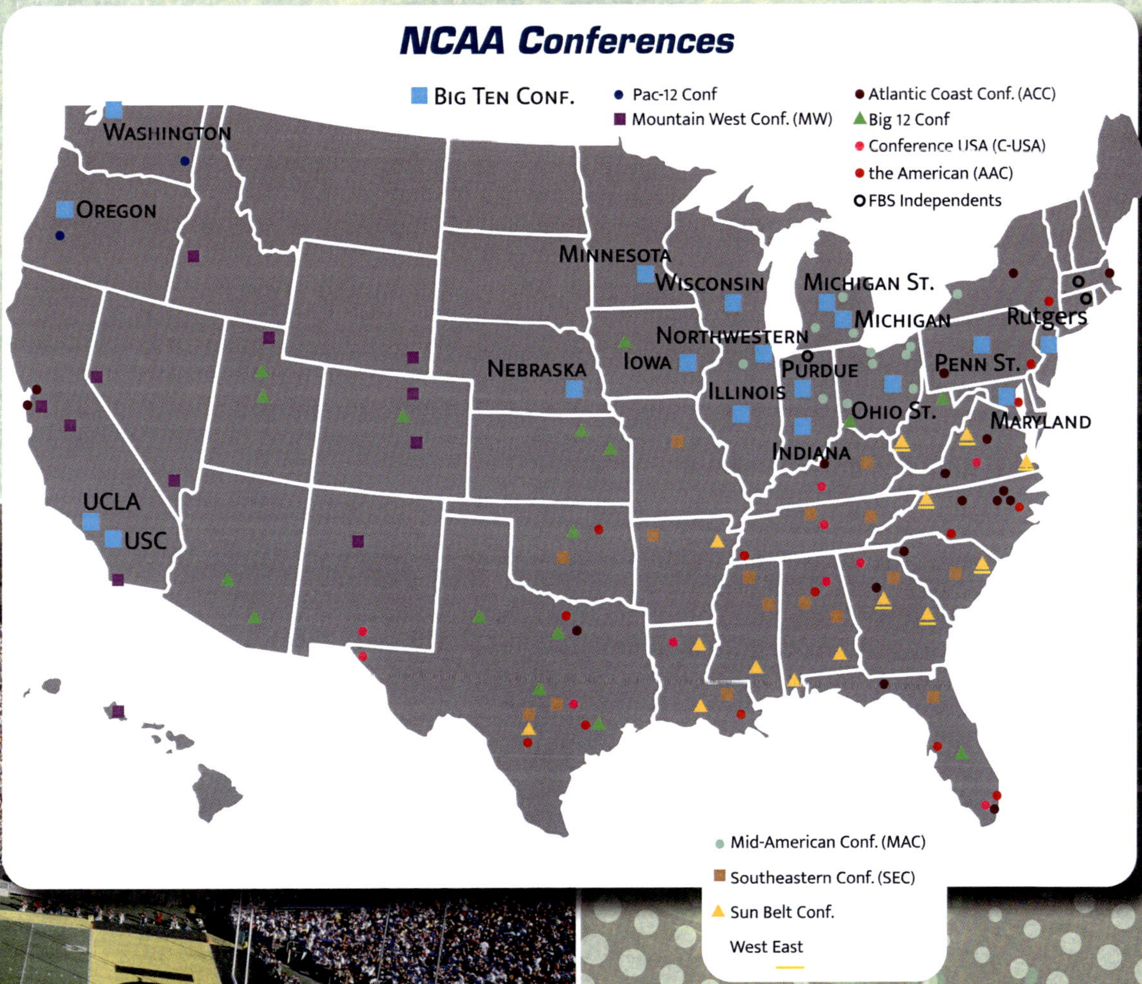

## Bowl Games

Bowl games are **postseason** games played by college teams based on their performance during the regular season as well as by their membership in different conferences. The highest-ranked conference champion teams compete in playoffs. Over the years, dozens of smaller bowls have come and gone. Today, there are almost 40 bowls that schools take part in. The six major bowl games, called the New Year's Six, are played on or near New Year's Day.

*The Famous Idaho Potato Bowl takes place in Boise, Idaho. It's played on artificial blue-colored turf, and there's a popular myth that it attracts waterfowl that believe it's a lake!*

## Bowl History

The first bowl game took place in 1902 as part of a sports festival called the Tournament of Roses in Pasadena, California. When the Rose Bowl stadium opened in 1923, the Tournament of Roses became known as the Rose Bowl. By 1935, other cities had begun hosting college bowls, and the number grew. The most famous are the New Year's Six: the Rose Bowl; the Sugar Bowl in New Orleans; the Orange Bowl in Miami Gardens, Florida; the Cotton Bowl in Arlington, Texas; the Fiesta Bowl in Tempe, Arizona; and the Peach Bowl in Atlanta, Georgia.

*The Rose Bowl Stadium, with room for nearly 93,000 fans, is the biggest, as well as the oldest, college bowl stadium.*

*The Orange Bowl trophy really is a bowl full of oranges. The game and parade are held in Miami, Florida.*

## National Champs

Though bowl games could be considered college football's championships, the NCAA has never held an official championship series. As a result, there have been different attempts by other groups to determine a national champion. The longest running of these is a poll taken by the Associated Press. This poll, taken since 1936, is voted on by sportswriters from all over America. The vote began due to the fact that in many different conferences and divisions top teams were not able to meet in bowl games.

*The **Heisman Trophy** has been college football's top individual award since 1935. It is named for John Heisman, a hall-of-fame coach.*

## The Knockouts

From 1998 to 2013, the Bowl Championship Series (BCS) took up the challenge of trying to establish a national champion. Using a combination of poll results and computer-determined standings, the top NCAA teams were invited to the top bowl games. The top two teams selected would play in the BCS National Championship Game, which rotated from participating bowl to bowl annually. In 2015, this complicated system was replaced by the College Football Playoff (CFP). This new system, which was in effect until 2023, was made up of a committee of 13 people who voted on the top four teams from the NCAA's top division. These teams were paired off for two semifinal games, with the winners facing off in the College Football Playoff National Championship.

2024
NATIONAL CHAMPIONSHIP

*In 2024, the University of Michigan Wolverines won the last four-team CFP National Championship. The following year the championship was expanded to a 12-team format.*

## Traditional Rivalries

Traditional rivalries in college football go back as far as the 1890s. The winning school takes home bragging rights and often a unique trophy. Most colleges have at least one big rivalry, and fans root against their school's **rival** no matter who they are playing! Some of the biggest rivalries involve schools that are closely located near each other. The annual game between the University of Michigan Wolverines and their Midwest neighbors, the Ohio State Buckeyes, is considered one of the fiercest of college football's many rivalries.

*For over 80 years, the University of Southern California (USC) and University of California Los Angeles (UCLA) have played for the Victory Bell, a brass bell that once chimed from a locomotive.*

*The Notre Dame-USC football rivalry, which began in 1926, is considered one of the most important in college football.*

## Bowl History

Despite the huge distance between them, the Fighting Irish of Notre Dame University in Indiana and the Trojans of the University of Southern California have become huge rivals. Both schools have top football programs and fans all over the country, so their games draw a big audience on television. The winner is awarded the Jeweled Shillelagh, a traditional Irish wooden club that bears the name of the winning team from every game.

## Army-Navy

Once a year, teams from the United States Military Academy (USMA) and the United States Naval Academy (USNA ) meet in the famous Army-Navy Game. The game is the final scheduled game of the major college football season, and has been played for more than 125 years.

CHAPTER 3

# THE RISE OF THE NFL

**When football first started, there were no professional players or athletes who were paid to play. In fact, there were rules against paying athletes. Some athletic clubs got around these rules by obtaining jobs for their players, or by giving them expensive gifts that they could sell for cash.**

## Going Pro

In 1892, William "Pudge" Heffelfinger became the first person to play the game for cash when he received $500 to play for the Allegheny Athletic Association against the Pittsburgh Athletic Club. Another one of the first players to accept money to play was John Brallier, who was paid $10 plus expenses to play a game for the Latrobe Athletic Association in Pennsylvania in 1895.

*Heffelfinger played for Yale from 1888–1891 before graduating in 1892.*

*Latrobe was also the first team to play a season with a team made up entirely of paid professional players, in 1897.*

## Going Pro

In 1899, an independent pro team calling themselves the Morgan Athletic Club started up in Chicago. After a series of name changes, they eventually became the Chicago Cardinals, and after a few moves, they ended up in Phoenix. Today they're known as the Arizona Cardinals, making them the oldest pro team still playing in the NFL. Other independent pro teams followed, with Ohio having as many as seven teams at once!

*The Chicago Cardinals, along with the Chicago Bears, were the first members of the NFL in 1920.*

### A Scandal!

When money is involved, things can get messy quickly. The sport's first major scandal happened in Ohio in 1906. The Canton Bulldogs coach and a Massillon Tigers player were accused of trying to fix games by getting one team to lose on purpose. Then, anyone who was part of the scam could bet money on the other team to win. Although nothing was ever proven, fans felt betrayed and abandoned the two teams, leading to them being shut down.

*Jim Thorpe was voted the American Professional Football Association's first president.*

## Early Leagues

As more independent teams emerged, small **regional** leagues began to form around them. With its large number of teams, one of the biggest of these local leagues was the Ohio League. By 1920, these early leagues were facing a few problems, such as growing player salaries and top athletes hopping from team to team for better offers.

Teams were also recruiting college players before they had even graduated. Hoping a strong national league, similar to baseball's, would solve these issues, representatives from five teams met at a Hupmobile auto dealership on August 20, 1920, in Canton, Ohio. This meeting resulted in many of the Ohio League teams forming the American Professional Football Conference. Within a month, teams from Illinois, New York, and Indiana had been recruited, and the name was changed to the American Professional Football Association (APFA).

The founder of the Chicago Bears, George Halas (above) was nicknamed "Papa Bear." He won six championships in 40 years of owning and coaching his team.

## Early NFL

The league was renamed the National Football League two years later. Two of the first NFL teams, the Green Bay Packers and Chicago Bears, have built up a rivalry as fierce as any in college football. They first played in 1921, and now meet at least twice a year as divisional rivals in the NFL. Fans always expect the games to be rough because both teams have proud traditions of winning. Green Bay has won 13 NFL championships while Chicago has nine.

*The Green Bay Packers joined the league in 1921. The Packers are the only team in the NFL that is a publicly owned company. That means they are not owned by one person or another company. Over 100,000 people own shares in the team—even fans!*

## League Competition

For decades after its founding, the NFL continually faced competition from other leagues. One of the most popular of these smaller leagues was the All-America Football Conference (AAFC), which had its first season in 1946. However, despite having strong teams, the AAFC was not financially stable. It shut down in 1949, and the NFL absorbed three of its most popular teams, the Cleveland Browns, the Baltimore Colts, and the San Francisco 49ers. The 49ers were now the second NFL team representing the western United States, following the addition of the Los Angeles Rams in 1946.

### FAST FACT

**Wisconsin and Minnesota are top cheese-producing states. NFL training camps held in those states became known as the Cheese League. In the 1990s, foam cheese hats became a favorite way for fans to show their support.**

## More Growth

Just like in college football, the NFL decided to divide its teams into divisions and then conferences. By 1953, the NFL had 12 teams. Cleveland Browns, New York Giants, Philadelphia Eagles, Pittsburgh Steelers, Chicago Cardinals, and Washington Redskins combined to create the Eastern Conference; while the Baltimore Colts, Chicago Bears, Green Bay Packers, Detroit Lions, Los Angeles Rams, San Francisco 49ers made up the Western Conference.

**Eastern Conference**

**Western Conference**

### The Forgotten Four

Though there was never an official ban, 1933 marked the last season Black players were present in the NFL for 12 seasons. Their absence finally ended in 1946, when the NFL's Rams agreed to **integrate** black players. The Rams signed Kenneth Washington and Woody Strode, and the Browns signed Marion Motley and Bill Willis.

## Greatest Game

A turning point for the league came in 1958. That year's championship game between the Baltimore Colts and the New York Giants is often called the "greatest game ever played." The Baltimore Colts and their star quarterback, Johnny Unitas, beat the New York Giants 23–17. The Colts' victory was the first ever to end in sudden death overtime, and Unitas's drive for the winning touchdown was a masterpiece of play-calling. The game was the first nationally televised championship, which left those who watched talking for days.

*Johnny Unitas, known as "The Golden Arm," set many records for passing.*

*With an audience of around 45 million, the 1958 championship was the beginning of the sport's massive rise in popularity throughout the country.*

## Super Bowl's Beginnings

Pro football gained many fans in the 1950s. For the first time, football could be enjoyed at home as more people began purchasing TV sets. As fans **clamored** for more teams, the American Football League (AFL) sprang up in 1960 to rival the NFL. Throughout the decade, the leagues competed for players and audiences. The two leagues agreed to a **merger** in 1966—completed in 1970. The leagues also agreed to hold a championship game at the end of each season between their respective number-one teams. This contest would come to be known as the **Super Bowl**. Super Bowls I to IV were actually between two separate leagues. After the merger was completed, the NFL was structured into two conferences: the National Football Conference, or NFC, which included most of the pre-merger NFL teams, and the American Football Conference, or AFC, which was made up of all of the former AFL teams, as well as three pre-merger NFL teams.

*The NFL champion Green Bay Packers defeated the AFL champion Kansas City Chiefs in the first Super Bowl, which was played in 1967.*

## Expanding the League

Since NFL teams give a city prestige, economic benefits, and civic pride, competition for **franchises** is fierce. Fans in Baltimore and St. Louis saw their teams depart for rival areas (Indianapolis and Phoenix.) The Cleveland Browns were set to move to Baltimore, but legal problems and angry fans led to a compromise—the team would move to Baltimore but Cleveland would keep the Browns name and get an expansion team.

*Since 1972, pro football has been more popular than Major League Baseball or college football. Fans have packed stadiums and the NFL has prospered financially.*

## Greatest Game

NFL teams sometimes use the threat of relocation to gain improvements for their facilities. Fans so feared the possibility of the Buffalo Bills moving to Toronto in the mid-2000s that city, county, and state officials agreed to pay the team $95 million for stadium upgrades, even though the Bills were already very profitable.

*A better scoreboard was part of the 2012 deal that kept the Bills playing at Buffalo's Ralph Wilson Stadium.*

## Hall of Fame Glory

There is no greater honor for an NFL player than to be chosen for membership in the Pro Football Hall of Fame. The HoF was located in Canton, Ohio, in 1963 to honor the place where the NFL's initial meeting was held. Players, coaches, officials, owners, and team employees can be inducted. Players must be retired for at least five years before they can be awarded the golden jacket that comes with induction.

PRO FOOTBALL HALL OF FAME CANTON, OHIO

CHAPTER 4

# THE SUPER BOWL

**The road to the Super Bowl is never easy. Teams prepare for the regular season with four preseason games in late summer. They start with a maximum of 90 players, but the team can only put 53 on the opening-day** roster. **Then, the team must survive a tough 16-game schedule that begins in early September.**

## *Road to the Bowl*

Each team plays eight home games. Since winning in an away stadium is always difficult, a team usually must win most of their home games to have any chance of qualifying for the playoffs or postseason.

*The Super Bowl, the NFL's yearly championship game, is one of the most popular sports events on Earth.*

## The Playoffs

January is playoff time in the NFL. Six teams from each conference, made up of four division winners and two wild card teams (clubs that did not win the division but still had excellent records), play to decide the Super Bowl contestants. The month kicks off with the Wild Card Weekend, with two games in each conference between wild card teams and conference opponents. The survivors advance into the divisional final and then the conference championship game a week later. After a week's rest for the newly crowned AFC and NFC champions, the two teams meet in the Super Bowl.

*Football players at all levels dream of winning the Super Bowl. The dream came true for the fourth time for the Kansas City Chiefs when they won Super Bowl LVIII in 2024.*

### FAST FACT

**Over 100 million people watch the Super Bowl game on TV. It is famous for its commercials which are like mini films!**

### *All Eyes on It*

The Super Bowl is the most-watched sporting event of the year and the most-watched television event in the United States. Some people even tune in just to see the commercials, which often feature big stars. Today, the cost for a single 30-second commercial during the Super Bowl is $8 million or more.

## Roman Numerals

Roman numerals have been used to number each Super Bowl game since 1971. This is mostly done to avoid confusion, as the main season and the Super Bowl happen in different years. For example, the Super Bowl for the 2023 season took place on February 11, 2024. It would be confusing to call it Super Bowl 2023, because it takes place in 2024, or to call it Super Bowl 2024, because it was for the 2023 season. Instead, it is called Super Bowl LVIII. The only exception is Super Bowl 50, which would have simply been the single letter L.

*Super Bowl LVIII was played in Allegiant Stadium in Paradise, Nevada. This was the first time a Super Bowl was played in the Las Vegas Valley area.*

## Halftime Show

Another popular aspect of the Super Bowl is the halftime show, which often includes popular music stars. Like the commercials, the halftime show often draws in viewers with no interest in the game itself. Many Americans think of the game as a national holiday, with people organizing annual parties around it. The Super Bowl is also popular internationally. The only event with a larger annual audience is the Champions League final, Europe's top soccer championship.

*The American R&B singer Usher headlined the halftime show during Super Bowl LVIII.*

## The Super Bowl Trophy

The winning team of the Super Bowl is awarded the Vince Lombardi Trophy. Originally called the World Professional Football Championship Trophy, the design was first drawn on a napkin by the vice president of Tiffany & Co. during a lunch with then-NFL commissioner Pete Rozelle. In 1970, four years into its life, the trophy was renamed the Vince Lombardi Trophy after the legendary Green Bay Packers coach. Unlike hockey's Stanley Cup, a new Vince Lombardi Trophy is produced by Tiffany & Co. each season. While it is made of sterling silver, the trophy is pretty light. It weighs only seven pounds (3 kg).

CHAPTER 5

# AROUND THE GLOBE

**Gridiron, or American, football is played throughout the world, with players often starting in youth and school leagues—especially in the U.S. and Canada.**

## Different Rules

In the U.S., American football ranks as the country's most popular sport—higher than baseball, basketball, hockey, or soccer. In Canada, hockey has the greatest number of fans, followed by football, baseball, basketball, and soccer. Canadian football has slightly different rules than American football. It is known for its use of 12 players, a larger field, and more attempts to move the ball forward.

*The Toronto Argonauts of the CFL have played under the same name since 1873—a record for North American pro football teams.*

**FAST FACT**

**The Canadian Football League (CFL) was officially established in 1958, but there were other leagues before then.**

## CFL Teams

By the 1920s, pro football teams had formed in several Canadian cities. They played each other regularly, but did not form an official league until 1958, when the Canadian Football League (CFL) began. The CFL is a nine-team league, with the BC Lions, Edmonton Elks, Calgary Stampeders, Winnipeg Blue Bombers, and Saskatchewan Roughriders in the Western Division. The Eastern Division is home to the Hamilton Tiger-Cats, Toronto Argonauts, Ottawa Redblacks, and Montreal Alouettes.

*Since 1948, neighboring teams Toronto and Hamilton have played a huge rivalry game every September called the CFL's Labour Day Classic.*

## Canadian Football Field

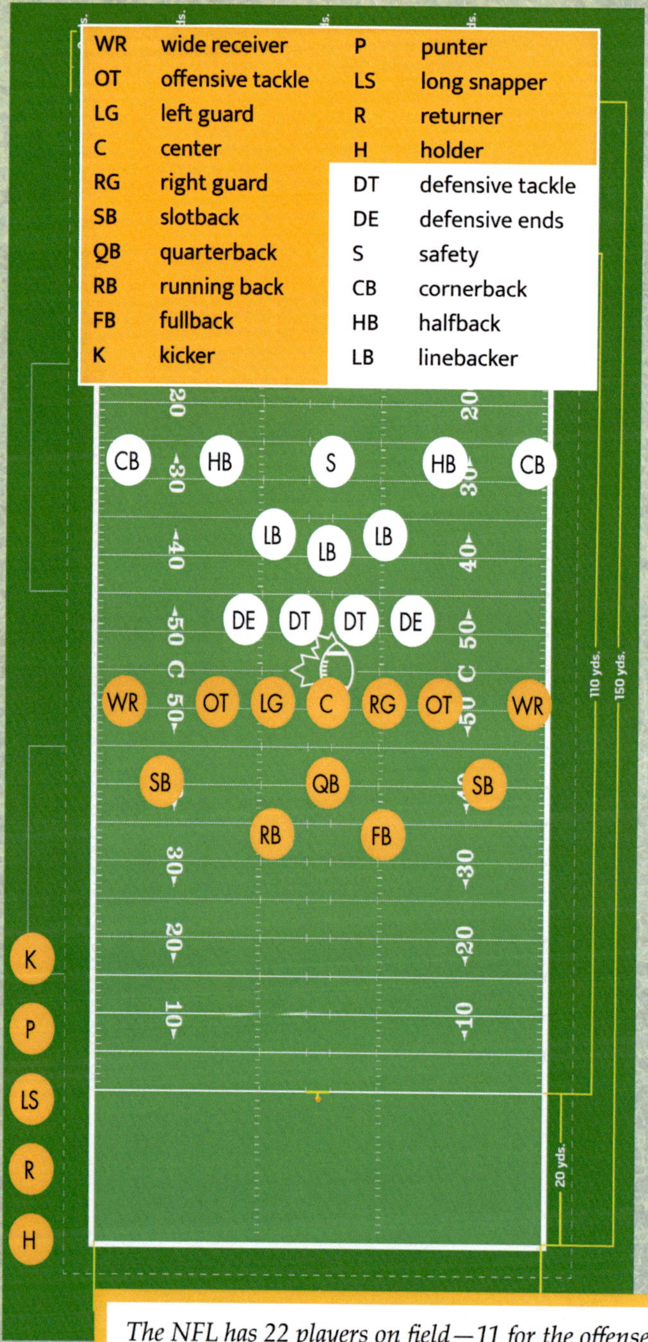


*The NFL has 22 players on field—11 for the offense and 11 for the defense. In the CFL, the total is 24—12 on offense and 12 on defense. CFL* ***end zones*** *are 20 yards (18 m) instead of 10 (9 m).*

## Game Rules

There are game differences and similarities between the NFL and the CFL. The most important is the number of downs. In the NFL, a team has four chances to gain 10 yards and a first down. The Canadian game features three downs in which a team can gain another first down, score a touchdown, or kick either a **field goal** or a single point. CFL fields are longer and wider. With fewer downs, the CFL game is more passing oriented. The CFL has a game-rule ratio, or formula, that says 21 players on a team of 45 must be "Nationals," or Canadian. That rule can be met in many ways, including if a player has one Canadian parent. Most of the other players are American—up to a maximum of 19.

## The Grey Cup

The **Grey Cup** is the CFL's annual championship game. The winners of each division in the CFL play for the Cup on the last Sunday in November. It's a big deal, with thousands of fans flocking to the host city for a week of parties. Millions more watch the game on TV. The CFL plays 18 regular-season games, then three weeks of playoffs. The first-place teams in each division get a week off, while the second- and third-place teams play to see who will advance. If a fourth-place team from one division has a better record than a third-place team from the opposite division, the team with the better record "crosses over" into the other division playoff.

*The CFL uses a replica as well as the original Grey Cup to save on wear and tear. Together, the two Cups have been broken six times, stolen twice, and damaged in a fire.*

## Earl Grey's Trophy

Made in 1909 for Albert Grey, Canada's **Governor General** at the time, the Grey Cup was originally intended to be donated to Canada's amateur hockey championship. However, another cup was donated for that purpose before his was ready. Earl Grey then gave the trophy for amateur rugby football. It was used on and off for decades, until the establishment of the CFL. It became both the trophy and the namesake of the league's championship game.

## European Game

American football has crossed over to Europe in the last 100 years or so, where the game has become very popular. Many Europeans got a good look at the game when they saw American and Canadian soldiers playing their versions of football on military bases during and after **World Wars I and II**. Starting in the 1970s, football began to take off in Europe. Europe has more than 2,000 teams playing American-style football, in leagues that range from youth to adult.

*In Europe, the Vienna Vikings have won five Eurobowl championships and finished as runners-up another five times in their 40-plus year history. In 2022, they became members and won the championship of the new European League of Football. They now go by the name Dacia Vienna Vikings.*

## European League

The European League of Football (ELF) is Europe's most recent professional football league. The league officially kicked off its first season in June 2021 with 16 teams located in nine countries across Europe. Currently, it has teams in Germany, Austria, Spain, Italy, Hungary, Poland, Switzerland, France, and the Czech Republic. There are plans to expand the league.

*The Frankfurt Galaxy were the league champions in the ELF's first season in 2021.*

## NFL Abroad

In an effort to boost its popularity in Europe and around the world, the NFL launched the NFL International Series. This is a number of regular season games played mostly in European cities. The first game in the International  Series took place in London in 2007, where theNew York Giants faced off against the Miami Dolphins. Since then, games featuring different NFL teams have been played in Mexico, Germany, Ireland, Spain, Brazil, and Australia.

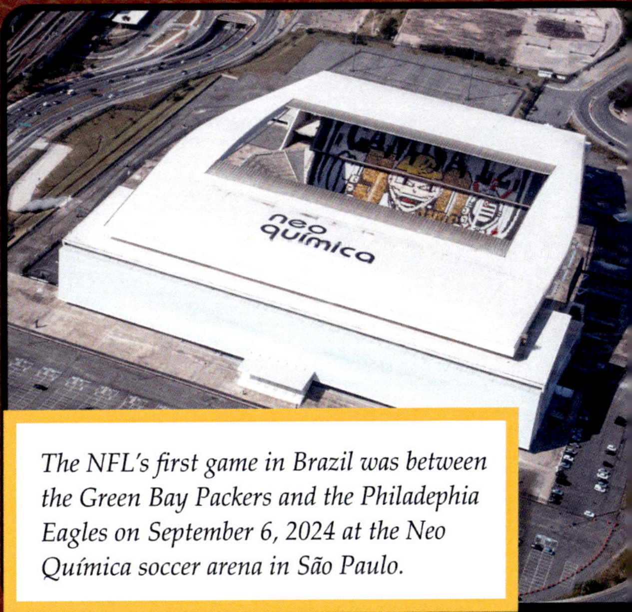


*The NFL's first game in Brazil was between the Green Bay Packers and the Philadephia Eagles on September 6, 2024 at the Neo Química soccer arena in São Paulo.*

CHAPTER 6

# HEROES AND SUPERSTARS

**Football is more than a game. At top levels, it's a business. It's also part of the culture that influences how people dress, talk, and think. Football's heroes and hall of famers are its superstars.**

**FAST FACT**

**The Pro Football Hall of Fame inducts coaches, owners, managers, and officials as well as players.**

## *Jim Brown, Renaissance Man*

Hall-of-fame fullback Jim Brown took the game to new heights. In 1957, his first season after being drafted by the Cleveland Browns, he led the league in **rushing** yards (942) and was named Rookie of the Year and league **MVP**. He went on to earn the MVP title three more times (1958, 1963, and 1965). Brown averaged over 100 yards per game and was the first player to make 100 rushing touchdowns. No matter how hard he was hit, Brown kept going. He didn't miss a single game or **Pro Bowl** in all of his nine seasons.

*Jim Brown was also a civil rights activist who spoke out against racial inequality in the 1950s and founded a union to encourage Black entrepreneurs in the 1960s. He played eight years (1957–65) and retired from football at age 30 for a career in acting.*

## The Golden Arm

It's hard to believe that hall-of-fame QB Johnny Unitas wasn't always recognized as one of the best players on the gridiron. Even the Pittsburgh Steelers, who chose him in the ninth round of the 1955 draft, didn't know what they had. They cut him from the team before he ever played a game. "Johnny U" played **semipro** that season. The next year, the Baltimore Colts signed Unitas as a backup. When the starting QB got injured in the fourth game, Unitas—who would soon be known as "The Golden Arm"—came out to play. Over his 17 years with the team, the three-time league MVP went on to set many records, including making at least one touchdown pass in eahc of 47 consecutive games.

*The 1958 championship game in which Unitas helped the Colts beat the New York Giants in overtime has been called "the greatest game ever played."*

*The 49ers drafted Joe Montana in 1979 and retired his number (16) in 1997. Montana was inducted into the Hall of Fame in 2000.*

## Offensive Leaders

Quarterbacks are like generals leading an army. They have amazing game sense and call the plays. They know the playbook inside and out, and can read the field to make split-second decisions about strategy. Superstar QBs are often recognized for their fast feet and powerful, accurate throwing arms. Nicknamed "Joe Cool" for his ability to stay calm when he was losing, quarterback Joe Montana (active 1979–1994) helped his first NFL team, the San Francisco 49ers, come from behind to win in the fourth quarter a mind-blowing 31 times. People called his power to pull off these comebacks "Montana Magic." One of the most memorable moments took place in 1989 during Super Bowl XXIII against the Cincinnati Bengals. With his team losing by six points and less than a minute to go in the game, Montana drove the ball 92 yards for a winning touchdown. "The Comeback Kid" earned a total of four Super Bowl victories and was MVP in three of them. He achieved many career playoff records and retired playing with the Kansas City Chiefs.

## QB Dynasty

Peyton Manning's family tree has some footballs hanging on it. His father, Archie, was a pro quarterback and his brother, Eli, was QB for the New York Giants. Genetics may have played a role in Peyton's success, but hard work was the key. While getting an education at the University of Tennessee, Peyton studied and memorized the playbook and **game film** to learn everything he could. In 1998, the Indianapolis Colts chose Peyton with the first overall draft pick. The QB with the cannon arm led the team to a win in Super Bowl XLI in 2007, and he took home game MVP. After 13 outstanding seasons with the Colts, Peyton missed the 2011 season while recovering from neck surgery, and was released from the team. Never one to give up, he signed with the Denver Broncos in 2012. He went on to be named Comeback Player of the Year and set many team records. Peyton received his fifth league MVP award in 2013.

*Peyton Manning finished his career after receiving his second Super Bowl ring for leading the Broncos to win Super Bowl 50 in 2016.*

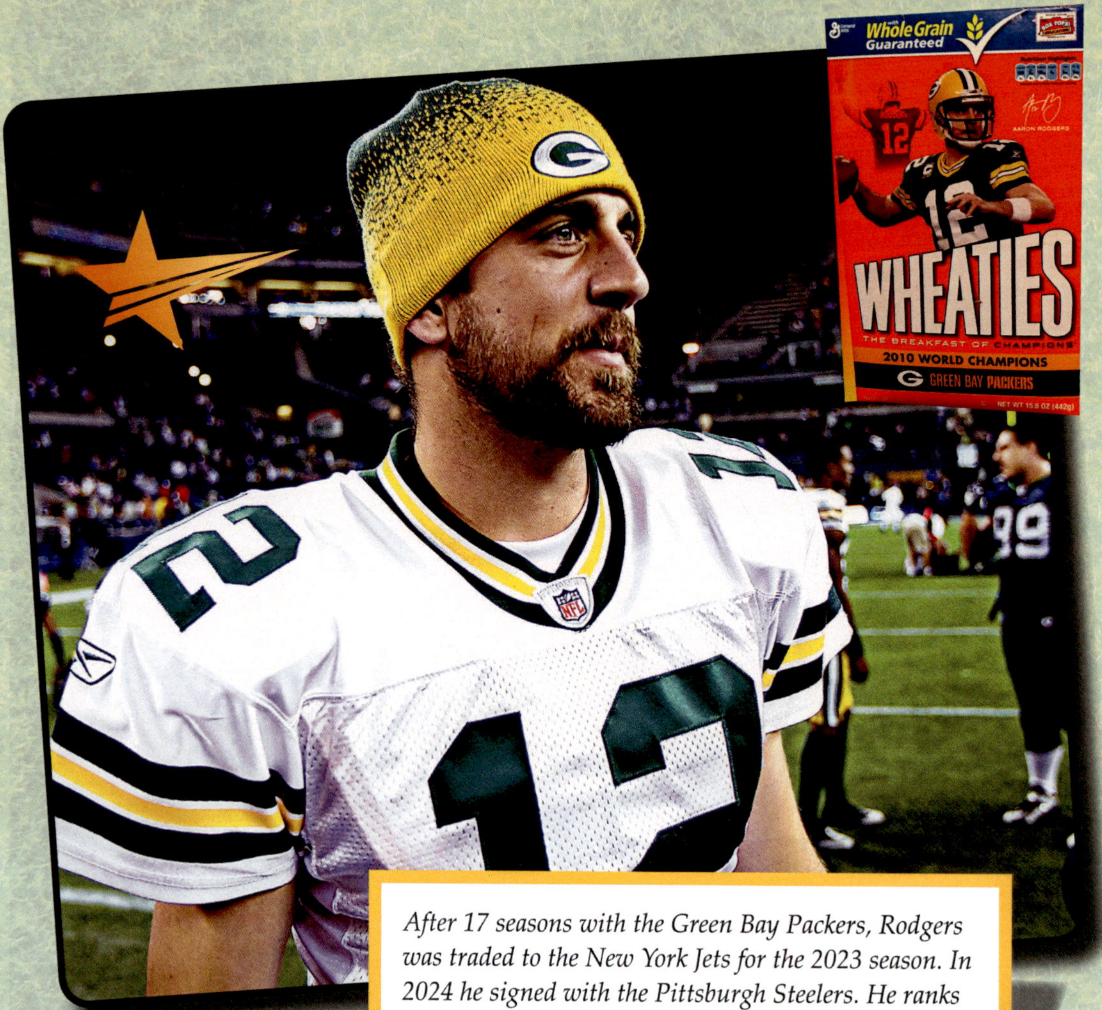


*After 17 seasons with the Green Bay Packers, Rodgers was traded to the New York Jets for the 2023 season. In 2024 he signed with the Pittsburgh Steelers. He ranks as one of the league's all-time career passers.*

## Aaron Rodgers

Aaron Rodgers was a star QB in high school, but he wasn't heavily recruited by the big football universities. He was patient. After playing for a year at community college, he transferred to the University of California, Berkeley, and was a Heisman finalist in 2004. His patience was tested again after the Green Bay Packers drafted him in 2005. In his first three seasons, he was backup QB to starter Brett Favre, and only played seven games. When Favre was traded in 2008, Rodgers finally got his chance. He helped lead the team to a Super Bowl XLV win in 2011 and was named league MVP. He went on to win three more NFL MVP awards in 2014, 2020, and 2021.

## Tom Brady

Tom Brady spent most of his rookie season in 2000 on the bench as backup QB for the New England Patriots. When the team's starter was injured in 2001, Brady was able to show that he had one of the best arms in football. Regarded as one of the greatest NFL players in history, he went on to earn seven Super Bowl rings and shatter many NFL records. He won a Super Bowl in three separate decades, the only quarterback in the NFL to do so. In 2020, at the age of 43, he received his fifth Super Bowl MVP, making him the oldest player to receive this award.

*Brady finished the last three years of his career (2020–2022) with the Tampa Bay Buccaneers where he led them to their second Super Bowl victory.*

## Madam Presidents

The NFL has women owners and co-owners, officials, coaches, negotiators, and vice presidents. But Sandra Douglass Morgan and Kristi Coleman made NFL history in 2022 when they became the first female presidents of NFL teams. Presidents are the teams top dogs who oversee all business aspects of the organization. Douglass Morgan of the Las Vegas Raiders is the first female Black and Asian president. Coleman is president of the Carolina Panthers.

## Acrobatic Wideouts

Wideouts have fast feet and good hands, meaning they can make unbelievable catches from the QB while running their play routes at track-star speed. The best of the best are focused, strong, and **agile**. They are able to anticipate plays and evade the best tacklers in the NFL by finding holes in their defense.

*Jerry Rice was elected to the Hall of Fame in 2010.*

After being drafted by the San Francisco 49ers in 1985, Jerry Rice played 20 incredible seasons in the NFL. The **wide receiver** was known for his dedication to preparing his body and mind to be the best on the field. He worked hard and his efforts paid off. Rice holds almost every career receiving record in the NFL, including receptions (1,549), receiving yards (22,895), and total touchdowns (208). Not surprisingly, Rice was named NFL MVP in 1987 and was selected to the Pro Bowl 13 times. He brought home three Super Bowl rings (1988, 1989, and 1994) during his 15 years with the 49ers, and went on to share his skills with the Oakland Raiders and Seattle Seahawks before retiring.

## Megatron

Calvin Johnson was one of the top draft picks in 2007. The two-time **All-American** at Georgia Tech wasn't a long shot. He performed amazingly in the **Scouting Combine** and had the perfect stats to play with the best. At 6'5" (1.96 m) and 239 pounds (108 kg), he ran the 40-yard dash in 4.35 seconds. In 2012, Johnson broke three NFL records in one night: single season receiving yards (1,964), consecutive hundred yard games (eight), and consecutive games with 10 or more receptions (four). Johnson was nicknamed Megatron after the fictional *Transformers* character. Johnson's amazing ability to run, leap, and catch have led him to be regarded as one of the best wide receivers of all time.

*Johnson retired from the Detroit Lions after the 2015 season and was inducted into the Hall of Fame in 2021.*

## Gronk

If Humpty Dumpty had the doctors, physiotherapists, and work ethic of New England Patriots' tight end Rob "Gronk" Gronkowski, he may actually have been put back together again. Considered one of the greatest tight ends of all time, Gronk had surgeries after suffering several injuries in 2012–13 to his back, left arm (broken twice), a concussion, and knee. This was after an amazing 2011 season, when the 6′6″ (1.98 m), 265-pound (120 kg) receiver set records for most **touchdown receptions** (17) and most receiving yards (1,327) by a tight end in a season. Gronkowski worked hard to recover from his injuries, and he surprised doctors and fans by coming back strong. In 2014, after taking on defense players like they were made of paper, he was named Comeback Player of the Year. That same year he helped his team win the Super Bowl. He went on to win two more Super Bowls with the Patriots and another with the Tampa Bay Buccaneers.

*After two seasons with the Tampa Bay Buccaneers, Gronk retired in 2022.*

*In 2021, Simon was hired as an assistant general manager for the Edmonton Elks.*

## CFL Hall-of-Famer

During Geroy Simon's 15 seasons as a **slotback** in the CFL, 12 of which he spent with the BC Lions, he was named to the Canadian All-Star team six times, won three Grey Cup championships, and was named the league's Most Outstanding Player in 2006. When he retired in 2014, Simon was the all-time career leader in CFL receiving yards with 16,352 yards. After retiring as a player, he became a scout, scouting director, and assistant general manager for several CFL teams. Later, he became general manager of the University of Maryland Terrapins football team.

## Polynesian Powerhouses

The NFL attracts players from all over the world, but those of **Polynesian** descent dominate. In fact, football players from the island country of Samoa in the South Pacific have a 1:20 chance of playing in the NFL. This is attributed to the Polynesian emphasis on community and self discipline. Most Polynesian players learn to play American football in school and the game becomes an opportunity to go to college and make it to the NFL.

*The Polynesian Football Hall of Fame, called Troy Palomao, was established in 2013 in Hawaii.*

## Leading Rushers

The best NFL players in this position use more than one weapon against defenders while carrying the ball down the field—speed to outrun them, agility to avoid them, and strength to break a tackle. Superstar running backs have the game vision to find a hole in the defense, and they can get there fast.

## Walter Payton

The Chicago Bears' first-round draft pick in 1975 has inspired all running backs that have come after him. Walter Payton's creative moves, including the "stutter-step" run that he developed in order to confuse tacklers, made him a force on the field. The hall-of-famer was also recognized for his speed, strength, agility (at times he leapt over his opponents!), and courage. His determination on the gridiron won him many NFL records over his 13 seasons with the Bears, including the single game rushing record of 275 yards.

*Payton was a Super Bowl XX Champ (1985), two-time NFL MVP, and nine-time Pro Bowler.*

## Marshawn Lynch

They called Marshawn Lynch "Beast Mode." He was known for besting would-be defenders by avoiding or running through them. In 2014, Lynch broke 101 tackles. He was relentless and often continued to gain yards even after contact. Surprisingly, Lynch's career started off rough. After being drafted by the Buffalo Bills in 2007, he didn't play as well as expected. In 2010, he was traded to the Seattle Seahawks. There, Lynch was trusted with over 23 carries per game by the end of 2011. "Beast Mode" went on to become an NFL rushing yards leader, five-time Pro Bowler, and a Super Bowl XLVIII Champion (2014).

*Lynch retired from the NFL three times! First in 2015, but he came back in 2017 for two seasons with the Oakland Raiders. He retired a second time, and came back in 2019 with the Seahawks for their last regular season game and playoff run. He then retired for a third and final time to become a co-owner of an indoor football team and an NHL team.*

### Legend of Women's Football

Linda Jefferson is one of only four women inducted into the American Football Association Hall of Fame. She ran for five consecutive 1,000-yard seasons. She helped her team, the Toledo Troopers of the National Women's Football League (NWFL), win seven consecutive national championships from 1971–1977.

## DeMarco Murray

DeMarco Murray was the NFL's top rusher, setting a franchise record for the Dallas Cowboys in 2014 (1,845 yards). This was outstanding, considering he was only drafted 71st in 2011. He has also beaten the record for most games with over 100 rushing yards in a season (12), and most single game rushing yards (253). The Cowboys trusted Murray enough to hand him the ball 392 times in 2014. That's why, in 2015, it came as a huge surprise (and disappointment) to many of his fans and teammates when Murray left the Cowboys to play for the Philadelphia Eagles. He spent one year with the Eagles before being traded to the Tennessee Titans. After a successful year with the Titans he earned his third Pro Bowler. The next year ended up being his last in the NFL when he retired from play.

*After seven seasons, Murray announced his retirement from the NFL in 2018. He became a college football coach and running back coach for the Kansas City Chiefs.*

## Jamaal Charles

Jamaal Charles is used to working hard and not giving up. As a child, he was diagnosed with a learning disability. Competing at the Special Olympics helped him prove that he had talent and skills. At the University of Texas, he proved that he could excel academically despite his learning disability. During his rookie NFL season, the Kansas City Chiefs barely used him (he rushed only 67 times). In 2009, the coach even listed Charles as inactive during a game when he was healthy. But, he showed them his worth. During each of the last four games that year, he rushed for 100 yards. He went on to become a four-time Pro Bowler, the Chiefs' rushing yards career leader, and the NFL career leader in average yards per carry (5.5).

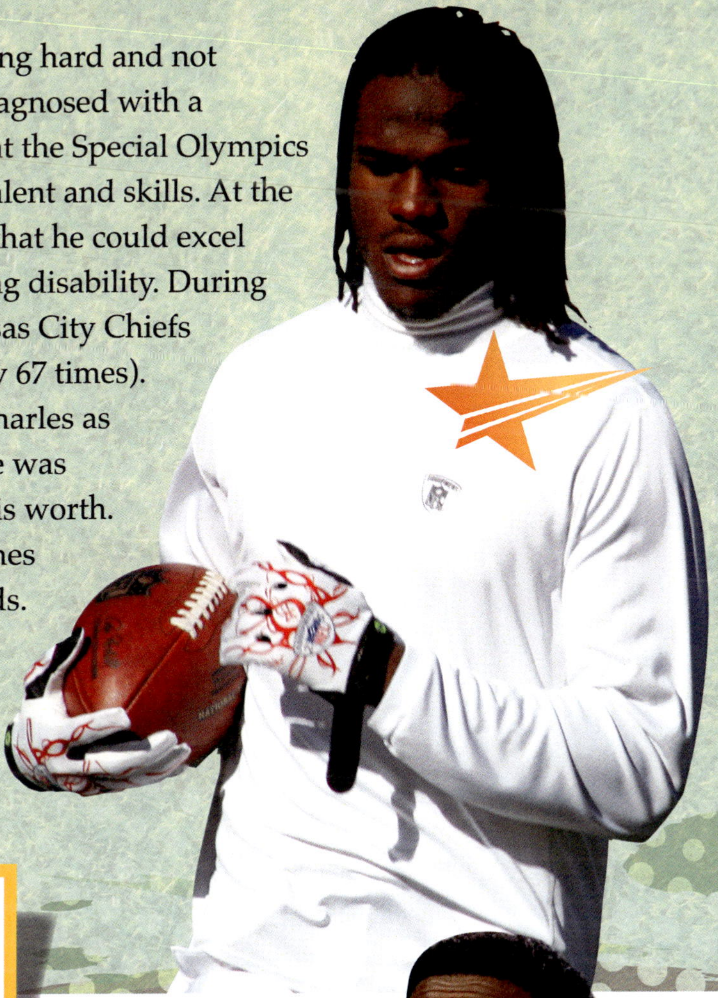

*Charles has won more Derrick Thomas Awards for being MVP of the Chiefs than any other player on the team.*

## Pinball Clemons

The CFL's Michael "Pinball" Clemons signed with the Toronto Argonauts in 1989. Before he retired in 2000, he racked up 12 all-time team records, including the pro football record for most combined yards in a career (25,438). He also won three Grey Cups as a player, one as head coach for the team, two as an executive, and one as a general manager.

## Outstanding Linemen

Offensive linemen (guards, tackles, and centers) are responsible for blocking for the QB and running backs, and creating holes in the opposition's defense so that pass plays and running plays can succeed. Defensive linemen (tackles and ends) stop the offense from blocking. They also tackle runners and try to take down the QB. Both offensive and defensive linemen are tough and big. Despite their size, they are also agile and fast on their feet.

### Joe Thomas

When Joe Thomas was up for the draft in 2007, he chose not to attend the event. He spent the day fishing with his dad on Lake Michigan instead. While catching trout, he also managed to reel in a spot as offensive tackle with the Cleveland Browns. Thomas was named to the Pro Bowl all but one of the 11 years he played. Thomas had 10,363 consecutive snaps played, the longest streak since the NFL began recording snap counts.

*Thomas was inducted into the Hall of Fame in 2023. He was the first Browns player inducted since their reactivation in 1999.*

## J.J. Watt

Quarterbacks were right to worry when they saw J. J. Watt standing on the opposite side of the line of scrimmage. The 2011 first-round draft pick for the Houston Texans is known as one of the top defensive ends of all-time. In 2014, the 6′5″ (1.96 m), 289-pound (131 kg) lineman became the first NFL player to complete a second season with more than 20 **sacks**. He also holds the Texans' record for **forced fumbles**. Not only did Watt prevent points, but he also earned them. Watt was known for picking off passes and returning for a touchdown. After he retired in 2022, Watt became a television analyst and announcer for football.

*In 2017, Watt was named Sportsman of the Year by* Sports Illustrated. *Watt's brothers T. J. and Derek were also NFL stars.*

In 2014, Houston was the NFL sacks leader with 22, which set a franchise single-season record, and won him the Deacon Jones Award for the player with the most QB sacks.

## Linebackers

You wouldn't want to mess with an athlete who plays this position. Running into a linebacker would feel a bit like hitting a brick wall. Not only are they strong, but the best linebackers can also quickly read the opposition's offense and direct the defensive play.

### Justin Houston

Looking back, it's clear that scouts underestimated Justin Houston's talent. It took until the third round of the 2011 draft for a team to call his name. While he had to wait for 69 players to be drafted ahead of him, it didn't take long for the Kansas City Chiefs to realize that they had signed one of the hardest-working players—and best defensemen—in the league. Once they had him, they didn't want to let him go. Houston's six-year contract extension worth $101 million made him one of the highest paid linebackers in NFL history. After eight seasons, the Chiefs released Houston. He moved to a couple of different teams before ending up with the Miami Dolphins in 2024.

## Luke Kuechly

Luke Kuechly started to play football in fourth grade. He became a linebacker and **safety** in high school, then moved on to play for Boston College where he nabbed NCAA tackling records before making his debut into the NFL in 2012 with the Carolina Panthers. In 2014, he led the NFL in tackles, was named Defensive Player of the Year, and won the Butkus Award for top linebacker in the league. Kuechly's amazing instinct for the game and great pass coverage ability also helped him to be named AP Defensive Rookie of the Year. His pro career ended in 2019 when he retired and took on the role of pro scout for the Panthers.

*Kuechly became a seven-time Pro Bowler before his retirement. He was elected to the Hall of Fame in 2026.*

## Most Feared Man

In his nine years as middle linebacker with the Chicago Bears, Dick Butkus developed a well-deserved reputation for playing hard that inspired fear in his opponents. Butkus was especially good at forcing fumbles. Other players were so wary of him that in 1970 *Sports Illustrated* featured him on its cover as "The Most Feared Man in the Game." The eight-time Pro Bowler made a career 1,020 tackles and was inducted into the Hall of Fame in 1979.

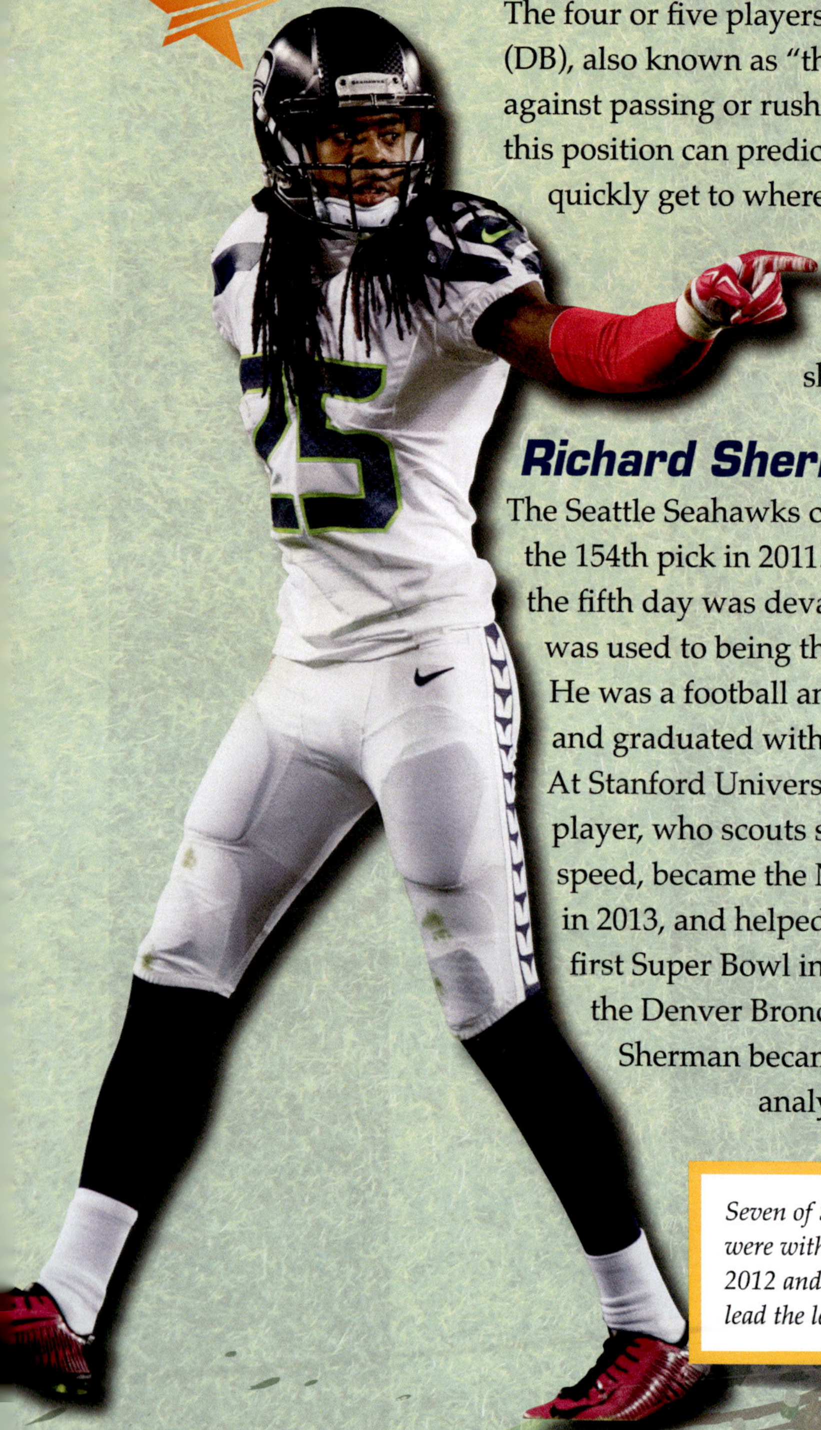

## Secondary Stars

The four or five players in the defensive backfield (DB), also known as "the secondary," protect against passing or rushing plays. Superstars in this position can predict offensive plays, and then quickly get to where they need to be. When the best DBs are on the field, opponents avoid their zone for fear of getting shut down.

## Richard Sherman

The Seattle Seahawks chose Richard Sherman as the 154th pick in 2011. Not being drafted until the fifth day was devastating for Sherman, who was used to being the best at anything he did. He was a football and track star in high school, and graduated with a 4.2 grade point average. At Stanford University he excelled again. The player, who scouts said lacked instinct and speed, became the NFL **interceptions** leader in 2013, and helped the Seahawks win their first Super Bowl in 2014 with a 43-8 win over the Denver Broncos. After retiring in 2021, Sherman became a pre-and post game analyst and podcast host.

*Seven of Sherman's eleven NFL seasons were with the Seattle Seahawks. Between 2012 and 2015, he helped the Seahawks lead the league in scoring defense.*

## Darrelle Revis

Cornerback Darrelle Revis named the area that he was defending on the gridiron "Revis Island," because opposing receivers often get stranded there without a ball ever thrown their way. Quarterbacks avoided throwing to his zone for good reason. Since 2007, Revis racked up 497 tackles, 29 interceptions, and 139 pass deflections. The 2015 Super Bowl XLIX champ was skilled at reading the offense, and he didn't wait for the opposing team to make their move. He took control. Off the field, he is quiet but equally gutsy.

*Revis is a seven-time Pro Bowler who played for the New York Jets, Tampa Bay Buccaneers, New England Patriots, and finished his career with the Kansas City Chiefs. He was inducted into the Hall of Fame in 2023.*

### The Champ

Roland "Champ" Bailey retired after 15 seasons in the NFL. He made his mark while playing for the Washington Redskins and Denver Broncos. Bailey was selected to play in 12 Pro Bowls, which is more than any cornerback in history.

# GLOSSARY

**agile** Being able to move quickly and easily

**All-American** Selected as one of the best in the U.S.

**clamored** Made a loud or strong demand

**downs** Chances for the team to advance the ball down the field

**end zone** The scoring area on either end of the football field

**expansion team** A new franchise, started from scratch, that begins play in the NFL

**field goal** A goal scored by kicking the ball through the goal posts

**first down** When the team gains 10 yards and gets another four or three downs

**forced fumble** When the ball carrier loses the football due to the force of a defensive player. This can be as a result of being hit or of having the ball stripped by a defender.

**forward pass** A pass thrown from behind the line of scrimmage toward the opponent's goal

**franchise** A team that is a member of a professional sports league

**Grey Cup** The championship game of the Canadian Football League (CFL

**Heisman Trophy** The award given to the most outstanding player in American college football

**integrate** To unite into a whole; to bring together different parts of society, such as races

**interception** When a defensive player catches the pass

**line of scrimmage** An imaginary line in football that marks the position of the ball at the start of each down

**mass-momentum** The combined force of a group of people or objects moving together

**Polynesian** An Indigenous member of Polynesia, a group of over 1,000 islands in the central and southern parts of the Pacific Ocean

**Pro Bowl** The all-star game of the National Football League (NFL)

**rival** One of two or more teams competing to see which one is the best; a traditional opponent

**roster** The official list of players on the team

**roughing the passer** Making illegal contact with the quarterback after the ball is released

**rushing** Gain of yards by running with the ball

**sack** When the quarterback (or another offensive player acting as a passer) is tackled behind the line of scrimmage before he can throw a forward pass

**safety** A defensive back who lines up 10–15 yards from the line of scrimmage

**Scouting Combine** An event where the best college players are invited to perform/try out in front of NFL coaches, scouts, and managers

**slotback** An offensive football halfback who lines up just behind the slot between an offensive end and tackle

**snap-back** Action in which the ball is thrown or handed backward by the center to a recipient

**Super Bowl** The championship game of the National Football League

**system of downs** Series of usually four downs in which a team must gain 10 yards to keep the ball; CFL has three downs

**tackle** When one player stops another, especially by knocking the opponent to the ground

**touchdown reception** When a player catches or receives the pass and then makes a touchdown

**wide receiver** An offensive player who is positioned at a distance from the end and is used primarily as a pass receiver

# LEARNING MORE

Check out these books and websites to learn everything about football.

## Books

Anastasio, Dina. *What Is the Super Bowl?* Penguin Random House, 2015.

Frederick, Shane. *The Best of Everything Football Book.* Capstone Press, 2011.

Jacobs, Greg. *The Everything Kids' Football Book: All-Time Greats, Legendary Teams, and Today's Favorite Players—with Tips on Playing Like a Pro*. Everything; 8th edition, 2024.

Sports Illustrated Kids. *Big Book of WHO Football*. Sports Illustrated, 2022.

## Websites

**www.profootballhof.com**
The Pro Football Hall of Fame has information about the history of football and the best football players of the past.

**www.cfhof.ca**
The Canadian Football Hall of Fame has information about the history of CFL football, as well as information on teams and players.

**www.nfl.com**
The official site of the NFL, this site features NFL standings as well as information on teams and players. Click on the video link to watch game highlights and catch up on all the latest news.

# INDEX